Garbage

Understanding Words in Context

Curriculum Consultant: JoAnne Buggey, Ph.D.
College of Education, University of Minnesota

By Robert Anderson

Greenhaven Press, Inc.
Post Office Box 289009
San Diego, CA 92198-0009

Titles in the opposing viewpoints juniors series:

Advertising	Male/Female Roles
AIDS	Nuclear Power
Alcohol	The Palestinian Conflict
Animal Rights	Patriotism
Causes of Crime	Population
Child Abuse	Poverty
Death Penalty	Prisons
Drugs and Sports	Smoking
Endangered Species	Television
The Environment	Toxic Wastes
Garbage	The U.S. Constitution
Gun Control	The War on Drugs
The Homeless	Working Mothers
Immigration	Zoos

Cover photo by: COMSTOCK INC./Robert Pastner

Library of Congress Cataloging-in-Publication Data

Anderson, Robert, 1950-
   Garbage: understanding words in context / by Robert Anderson;
curriculum consultant, JoAnne Buggey.
      p. cm. — (Opposing viewpoints juniors)
   Summary: Opposing viewpoints debate the seriousness of the garbage
crisis; whether incineration or recycling is the answer; and if
using cloth diapers will reduce the garbage problem. Vocabulary
exercises teach critical thinking and reading skills.
   ISBN 0-89908-609-8
   1. Refuse and refuse disposal—Juvenile literature.
2. Incineration—Juvenile literature. 3. Recycling (Waste, etc.)—
Juvenile literature. [1. Refuse and refuse disposal.
2. Pollution. 3. Vocabulary. 4. Critical thinking.] I. Buggey,
JoAnne. II. Title. III. Series.
TD792.A63   1991
363.72'8—dc20   91-22100
                                                                          CIP
                                                                          AC

CONTENTS

An Introduction to Opposing Viewpoints

When people disagree, it is hard to figure out who is right. You may decide one person is right just because the person is your friend or a relative. But this is not a very good reason to agree or disagree with someone. It is better if you try to understand why these people disagree. On what main points do they differ? Read or listen to each person's argument carefully. Separate the facts and opinions that each person presents. Finally, decide which argument best matches what you think. This process, examining an argument without emotion, is part of what critical thinking is all about.

This is not easy. Many things make it hard to understand and form opinions. People's values, ages, and experiences all influence the way they think. This is why learning to read and think critically is an invaluable skill. Opposing Viewpoints Juniors books will help you learn and practice skills to improve your ability to read critically. By reading opposing views on an issue, you will become familiar with methods people use to attempt to convince you that their point of view is right. And you will learn to separate the author's opinions from the facts they present.

Each Opposing Viewpoints Juniors book focuses on one critical thinking skill that will help you judge the views presented. Some of these skills are telling fact from opinion, recognizing propaganda techniques, and locating and analyzing the main idea. These skills will allow you to examine opposing viewpoints more easily.

Each viewpoint in this book is paraphrased from the original to make it easier to read. The viewpoints are placed in a running debate and are always placed with the pro view first.

Understanding Words in Context

Whenever you read, you may come across words you do not understand. Sometimes, because you do not know a word or words, you will not fully understand what you are reading. One way to avoid this is to interrupt your reading and look up the unfamiliar word in the dictionary. Another way is to examine the unfamiliar word in context, or by studying the words, ideas, and attitudes that surround the unfamiliar word.

In this Opposing Viewpoints Juniors book, you will be asked to determine the meaning of words you do not understand by considering their use in context.

Sometimes a word that has the same meaning as the unfamiliar word will be used in the sentence or in a surrounding sentence:

> Many animal species are **endangered** by human activities. Their lives are threatened by people destroying the environment.

The unfamiliar word is **endangered**. The clue is the word *threatened*. The second sentence is relating the same idea as the first sentence, but it is a little more specific. So, the words threatened and endangered should mean about the same thing. In fact, they do.

Often, the surrounding sentences will not contain a word similar to the unfamiliar word. They may, however, contain ideas that suggest the meaning of the unknown word:

> The United States has many **assets**. It has beautiful scenery, natural resources, generous people, and great wealth.

The meaning of the word **assets** can be determined by studying the ideas around it. Beautiful scenery, natural resources, generous people, and great wealth are all clues to the meaning of the word assets, things that are desirable to own.

In some cases, opposite words and ideas can offer the reader clues about an unfamiliar word:

> Seldom will you find a man with more than one wife. Most men are **monogamous**.

The unfamiliar word is **monogamous**. The clue is *more than one wife* in the first sentence. In this case, the author is saying, "You do not usually find a man with more than one wife, so you do usually find a man with only one wife." Monogamous, then, must mean "having only one wife."

Sometimes the meanings of unfamiliar words are more difficult to determine. You just have to pay attention to the meaning of the sentence to figure them out:

> Pickpockets can be **incapacitated** by cutting off their hands.

To determine what **incapacitated** means, you have to figure out that cutting off pickpockets' hands would stop them from picking people's pockets. So incapacitated must mean that a person cannot do something.

Sometimes you will not be able to determine what a word means by its context. You will have to look it up in a dictionary.

In the following viewpoints, several of the words are highlighted. You must determine the meanings of these highlighted words by studying them in context. As you read the material presented in this book, stop at the unfamiliar words and try to determine their meanings. Finally, use a dictionary to see how well you have understood the words.

We invited two students to give their opinions on the garbage issue. We asked each of them to look up an unfamiliar word and use it in a sentence. In the students' viewpoints and the ones on the following pages, try to figure out the meanings of words you do not understand.

Garbage is a big problem.

Everywhere I look, I see things that are supposed to be used once and then thrown away. At school we use **disposable** plates, cups, knives, forks, and spoons as well as paper napkins and towels. We throw away our pens and notebooks when we've finished with them. Then the janitor empties the trash cans into the big dumpsters behind the school building. Twice a week the dumpsters are emptied into a gigantic garbage truck that takes away the trash. My dad showed me the place outside town where the garbage trucks unload their garbage. It's called a landfill. There were huge mountains of smelly garbage there. He said that pretty soon there won't be room to dump any more garbage there. No one knows what we'll do with our garbage then.

Garbage is not a big problem.

I don't think garbage is such a big problem. We have plenty of room in this country to dump our garbage. And more and more people are recycling. At our house we have four bins on the back porch. One is for glass, one is for cans, one is for plastic, and one is for paper. We use the garbage disposal in the kitchen sink for food waste. So we only have to take out the trash about once a week.

My teacher said that soon most cities will have organized recycling programs and places where garbage can be burned to make electricity. These ideas are just a couple of **alternatives** to dumping garbage in a landfill. These other methods of dealing with garbage will keep garbage from ever becoming a big problem.

ANALYZING THE
SAMPLE VIEWPOINTS

Dustin and Sammi have very different opinions about the garbage problem. Both of them use words you might not understand. But you should be able to discover the meanings of these words by considering their use in context.

Dustin:

Everywhere I look, I see things that are supposed to be used once and then thrown away. At school we use *disposable* plates, cups, knives, forks, and spoons, as well as paper napkins and towels. We throw away our pens and notebooks when we've finished with them.

NEW WORD	CLUE WORD OR IDEA	DEFINITION
disposable	throw away	something that can be thrown away after use

Sammi:

These ideas are just a couple of *alternatives* to dumping garbage in a landfill. These other methods of dealing with garbage will keep garbage from ever becoming a big problem.

NEW WORD	CLUE WORD OR IDEA	DEFINITION
alternatives	other methods	other ways of doing something

Both Dustin and Sammi believe they are right about the garbage problem. Which student do you think is right? Why?

As you read the viewpoints in this book, keep a list of the new words you come across. Write down what you think the words mean from their context. Check your definitions against those in a dictionary.

CHAPTER 1

PREFACE: Is Garbage a Serious Problem?

"Sweeping dirt under the rug" is an old saying. It refers to covering up something instead of properly disposing of it. Some people believe this saying is an apt description of Americans' attitude toward garbage: dump it in a landfill and cover it up so we cannot see it. Then we will not have to worry about how much more we make.

Many people believe this attitude has led to a serious garbage problem. According to these people, Americans produce too much unnecessary waste—especially in the form of product packaging. Paper and plastic packaging surrounds almost everything sold in today's stores. Such packaging may make a product more attractive to the buyer, but it becomes needless waste later. These people also note that America's garbage dumps are filling up fast. Soon, they say, there will be nowhere to dump garbage. They warn Americans to stop producing unnecessary garbage before a serious problem becomes completely unmanageable.

Other people, however, do not see garbage as a serious problem. They note that throughout history people have met the challenge of disposing of their garbage. One researcher, William Rathje, states that Americans do not produce any more waste now than in the past. He does not believe that packaging is wasteful and unnecessary. On the contrary, he argues, packaging preserves food and prevents it from being wasted. Rathje and others like him contend that America can easily solve today's garbage problem.

The following two viewpoints debate the seriousness of the garbage problem. As you read, you may see words you do not understand. Try to determine the meaning of these words by their use in context. Keep a list of the new words you find.

Editor's Note: This viewpoint argues that America faces a serious garbage problem because places to dump garbage are becoming scarce. The author warns Americans to change their wasteful life-styles to reduce the amount of garbage created.

Americans throw away 160 million tons of trash each year. Imagine 1,000 football fields piled 30 stories high with trash. That is what the 160 million tons of garbage that we discard each year looks like. And the amount grows larger every year.

Garbage has become a serious problem. We are running out of places to put it. New York City's main garbage dump is the largest of any city in the world. Twenty-four thousand tons of garbage are dumped in it each day. By the year 2000, it will be larger than the Great Pyramid of Cheops in Egypt. It probably will not be open that long, though, since it is leaking **toxic** wastes into the groundwater. The city cannot risk poisoning the water supply, so the dump may be closed very soon. If it is closed, New York City will have nowhere to dump its huge volume of garbage. This possibility inspired the city's sanitation commissioner, Brendan Sexton, to greet newly elected mayor David Dinkins with the message: "Hi. Welcome to City Hall. By the way, you have no

The text tells you that *toxic* wastes poison the water supply. From this information, you can figure out that *toxic* means poisonous.

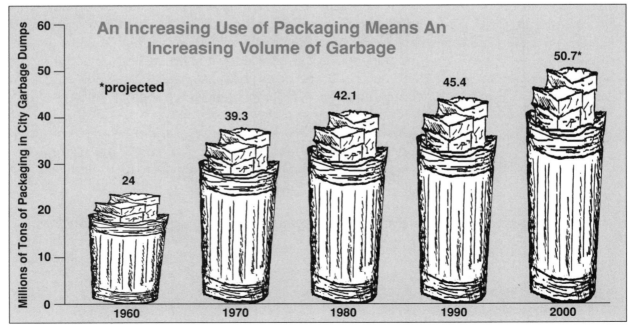

An Increasing Use of Packaging Means An Increasing Volume of Garbage

*projected

Millions of Tons of Packaging in City Garbage Dumps

1960 — 24
1970 — 39.3
1980 — 42.1
1990 — 45.4
2000 — 50.7*

Source: Franklin Associates, Ltd.

place to put the trash."

New York City is not the only place facing a garbage crisis. *Newsweek* magazine reports that more than two-thirds of America's landfills have closed since the late 1970s, and one-third of remaining landfills will be full by 1994.

Garbage does not seem like a big problem to most Americans. They just throw it away. Then the garbage truck picks it up, takes it somewhere, dumps it, and that is that. But there is too much garbage to get rid of. The **glut** of garbage and the **scarcity** of landfills in which to bury it have created a need for new sites for our garbage. The problem is *where* to locate new landfills. No one wants to live near a smelly, unsightly garbage dump full of **malodorous**, rotting trash.

Why is there so much garbage? A large part of the answer lies in the way we live. To have enough time to work, make a home, travel, and enjoy sports, music, and art, Americans use more and more disposable products. Throwing away paper dishes, paper towels, paper diapers, plastic bottles, and other plastic containers saves us time. The price we pay for this convenience is a growing garbage problem.

The problem of garbage may not be as glamorous as other environmental issues like the destruction of the Amazon Rain Forest, but its consequences can be just as serious. For example, even normal household garbage contains chemicals that can damage the environment. The "empty" chlorine bleach bottle Dad throws away probably still has a teaspoon or so of bleach in it. When Mom finishes painting the kids' playhouse, she throws away the rags, paint stirrers, and "empty" paint cans coated with paint. These items may seem harmless and insignificant. But multiply them by the millions of families living in the United States, and you begin to see great pools of bleach and gallons of paint leaking into the ground and the water under the ground. We must change our attitudes and life-styles, or **wallow** in our own waste.

Too much is the clue to the meaning of *glut*. If there is too much garbage but not enough landfills, what is a *scarcity* of landfills?

What are the clues to the meaning of *malodorous*? One clue is a word hidden within *malodorous* itself. Can you find it?

© Wicks/Rothco. Reprinted with permission.

Some words sound like what they mean. From its context and from how it sounds what does *wallow* mean?

Are more landfills needed?

This viewpoint claims that overflowing landfills are closing in many states. These states must find new sites for landfills, but people do not want to live near a landfill. Why not? What other solutions to the garbage problem are possible?

Editor's Note: This viewpoint argues that the problem of garbage is a false one created by the media. It points out that alternatives exist for disposing of garbage.

The text says the media have *fabricated* an image. The clue to the meaning of *fabricated* is in the next phrase which says the image was "made up." *Fabricated* means "made up."

The clue to the meaning of *statistics* is in the sentences that follow it. What are *statistics*?

The image of America drowning in a sea of garbage is a false one. The image has been **fabricated** by the media, which have made it up to sell newspapers and advertising time on news programs. Look around as people go to work or school or to the store. How often do you see landfills bulging with mountains of garbage that threaten to overflow their boundaries? Never! Where is all this garbage we should worry about? Most of it is in our minds, according to some researchers.

William Rathje is a University of Arizona scientist who studies garbage. He says that Americans believe they are more wasteful than they really are. They read and hear about how much packaging they use and how America has become a throwaway society more concerned about convenience than the environment. They see **statistics** showing that each American creates anywhere from three to eight pounds of garbage every day. But those numbers are too high, says Rathje. According to Rathje's research,

Danziger. Reprinted with permission.

even three pounds a day may be too high an estimate for many parts of the country.

As for all that packaging, its purpose is to protect and preserve food, and it has saved us from a lot of garbage in the form of food waste. For example, most people buy packaged orange juice made from concentrate instead of squeezing their own oranges for juice. If you think squeezing your own juice produces less waste, consider this: orange juice producers sell the leftover orange rinds for animal feed. Households do not. They throw the rinds away; that is, the rinds become garbage. Thus, we should not see packaged, concentrated orange juice as just a convenience for lazy Americans.

Americans also believe that they make more waste than people of poorer nations make. This is also a false image. According to studies done by the University of Arizona's Garbage Project, the average household in Mexico City produces 33 percent more garbage than an average American household. Why? Many food products in Mexico rot and become garbage before people can eat them. But packaging preserves American goods.

It is true that some densely **populated** areas, like the Northeast United States, have filled up most of the space they have set aside for garbage. These areas have so many people that there is no room for more garbage dumps. The leaders of these cities will have to think up **alternatives** to dumping garbage in a landfill. There are other ways to dispose of garbage besides dumping.

According to scientists who have studied the matter, people throughout history have solved their garbage problems in four ways: by dumping it, burning it, recycling it, and trying to make as little of it as possible. These four ways are still **adequate** for disposing of America's garbage, William Rathje argues. And they will be good enough for our needs far into the future as well.

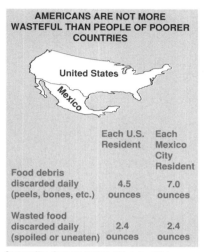

AMERICANS ARE NOT MORE WASTEFUL THAN PEOPLE OF POORER COUNTRIES

United States

Mexico

	Each U.S. Resident	Each Mexico City Resident
Food debris discarded daily (peels, bones, etc.)	4.5 ounces	7.0 ounces
Wasted food discarded daily (spoiled or uneaten)	2.4 ounces	2.4 ounces

Source: *The Garbage Project*, University of Arizona

Populated describes the word "areas" in this sentence. Look in the next sentence for a hint of the meaning of *populated*. What does *populated* mean?

Sammi used the word *alternatives* in her sample viewpoint. What does *alternatives* mean?

Can you figure out the meaning of the word *adequate* by its context? What are the clues to the meaning of *adequate*?

Do the media exaggerate problems?

Newspapers, magazines, TV, and radio inform people of events that happen around the world. If the media decide to report every story that comes along about garbage, people will hear and see a lot about it. The viewpoint's author thinks that people may then believe garbage is a more important issue than it really is. Do you believe everything you read in the newspaper or see on TV? Do you think you should? Why or why not?

Understanding Words in Context

The sentences below are adapted from viewpoints 1 and 2. Try to define each highlighted word by considering its use in context. You will find four possible definitions of the highlighted word under each sentence. Choose the definition that is closest to your understanding of the word. Use a dictionary to see how well you understood the words in context.

1. When the federal government threatened to close down New York City's overfull garbage dump, the city faced a severe garbage problem. The head of the city's **sanitation** department greeted the newly elected mayor with the message: "Hi. Welcome to City Hall. You have no place to put the trash."

   a. population   c. forestry

   b. waste disposal   d. mental illness

2. Empty paint cans and bleach bottles seem like harmless and **insignificant** items of garbage, but they add tons of toxic wastes to our country's volume of garbage.

   a. dangerous   c. sweet

   b. pretty   d. unimportant

3. The problem of garbage may not be as **glamorous** as oil spills or destroying rain forests, but its consequences can be just as serious.

   a. silly and odd   c. exciting and attractive

   b. small and weak   d. strong and powerful

4. New York City is not the only place facing a garbage **crisis**. *Newsweek* magazine reports that more than two-thirds of America's landfills have closed.

   a. a large formal affair with lots of flowers   c. a happening of little importance to anyone

   b. a sale of expensive art objects   d. a serious state of affairs needing a decision

5. Throwing away paper dishes, paper towels, paper diapers, and plastic bottles and other containers, saves us the time needed to clean, store, and maintain these necessary items. The price we pay for this **convenience** is a growing garbage problem.

   a. something made for easy, quick use   c. expensive furniture

   b. a new kind of storage container   d. small grocery store

CHAPTER

PREFACE: Would Burning Trash Reduce the Garbage Problem?

The amount of garbage in America is fast exceeding the amount of landfill space in which to dump it. City, state, and federal authorities are searching for ways to reduce the volume of trash. In this way, they hope to keep landfills open longer.

Many authorities and waste-disposal experts believe burning the garbage is the answer to this problem. Burning trash reduces its volume by 90 percent, leaving only a small amount of ash to be buried in a landfill. Burning garbage also produces energy that can be used to make electricity. Thus, burning seems to solve two problems at once: It reduces garbage volume and provides energy.

Some experts, however, reject burning as a solution to the garbage problem. Most environmentalists, for example, argue that the leftover ash is too poisonous to put in a landfill. They also claim that waste-burning plants are dangerous and cost too much to build. Opponents to burning believe that recycling and other methods of reducing trash are just as effective, yet safer.

The next two viewpoints debate the issue of whether burning trash would reduce the garbage problem. Watch for the highlighted words in the text. Try to determine the meaning of these words from their context.

Editor's Note: This viewpoint argues that burning trash in waste-to-energy plants reduces waste, provides energy, and is a safe, affordable disposal method.

Can you find the clues to the meaning of *minimize* in the words and ideas around it? What do you think *minimize* means here?

From its context, can you determine the meaning of *residual*? What does *residual* mean?

A shortage of landfill space is the core of America's garbage problem. We produce more and more garbage, but we have less and less room to use for landfill sites. The best way to solve this problem is to **minimize** the amount of garbage we put into landfills. The less we bury in landfills, the longer it will take to fill them, and the longer we can use them.

How can we put less into our landfills? By first burning our solid wastes. Burning garbage leaves only a small amount of ash to dispose of in a landfill. Burning our trash in specially built waste-burning plants would reduce the volume of waste dumped into landfills by 90 percent.

Many people are opposed to burning garbage. They are afraid that the **residual** ash is harmful to the environment and to people. But the U.S. Environmental Protection Agency (EPA) has tested the ash from garbage that has been burnt in specially built waste-burning plants. It has almost always found the ash to be safe. The only times the ash has failed the EPA's tests are when the ash contains poisonous metals like cadmium or lead. Even so, the ash

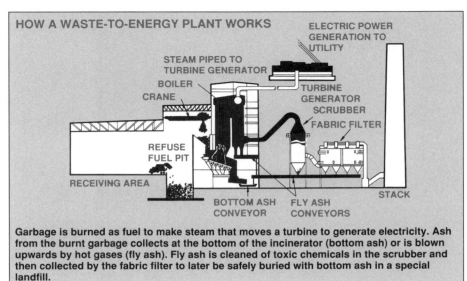

HOW A WASTE-TO-ENERGY PLANT WORKS

ELECTRIC POWER GENERATION TO UTILITY

STEAM PIPED TO TURBINE GENERATOR

BOILER

CRANE

TURBINE GENERATOR

SCRUBBER

FABRIC FILTER

REFUSE FUEL PIT

RECEIVING AREA

BOTTOM ASH CONVEYOR

FLY ASH CONVEYORS

STACK

Garbage is burned as fuel to make steam that moves a turbine to generate electricity. Ash from the burnt garbage collects at the bottom of the incinerator (bottom ash) or is blown upwards by hot gases (fly ash). Fly ash is cleaned of toxic chemicals in the scrubber and then collected by the fabric filter to later be safely buried with bottom ash in a special landfill.

Source: Wheelabrator Environmental Systems Inc. Reprinted with permission.

contains about twenty times less of these metals than unburnt trash does, according to Harold Draper. Draper is a scientist for the Tennessee Valley Authority, a U.S. government organization that oversees electric-power production in the Tennessee River Valley. The simple truth is that the ash of **incinerated** waste contains nothing that was not there before the waste was burnt.

Many people imagine garbage-burning plants to be dirty places with great smokestacks belching air-polluting smoke and ash into the air. They believe these plants are just like the old backyard incinerators in which people used to burn their household garbage and which the government banned in the early 1970s. But modern incineration plants are very high tech. They do not pour smoke and polluting gases into the air. They filter out pollutants first.

Another benefit of incineration is that burning garbage produces heat, which can be used for energy. A city with a waste-burning plant not only can dispose of its garbage in a safe manner, but it can also produce energy to light its streets and run its computer systems. Two problems can be solved at once: garbage disposal and energy production—and at a very low cost. In fact, according to Harold Draper, waste-to-energy plants can **stabilize** waste disposal costs for more than twenty years. Anything that can level off the ever-rising costs of waste disposal should be welcomed by the American people.

Taylor also notes that Europe and Japan use waste-to-energy plants. Neither of these regions has a choice between dumping and burning. They have no room left in which to dump. Both need to **generate** more energy for themselves rather than having to buy it from other countries. Also, both Europe and Japan are very aware of the need to preserve the environment. They would not use a system that threatens the ecology. Americans that doubt the usefulness or safety of burning garbage might learn from the Europeans and the Japanese that burning garbage is a good way to reduce our garbage problem.

What is the word that gives the meaning of *incinerated* in this sentence? What does *incinerated* mean?

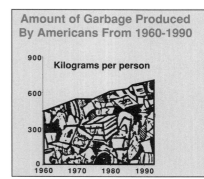

Amount of Garbage Produced By Americans From 1960-1990

Kilograms per person

900

600

300

0

1960   1970   1980   1990

Source: U.S. Environmental Protection Agency

What does the context of *stabilize* tell you about its meaning? What word or idea is the clue to the meaning of *stabilize*?

Determine the meaning of *generate* from its use in context. What does *generate* mean?

Are waste-to-energy plants a good idea?

Why might people fear a waste-burning plant operating in their community, according to this viewpoint? What does the viewpoint say are the rewards for burning trash before burying it in a landfill?

Burning trash would not reduce the garbage problem

> **Editor's Note:** The following viewpoint argues that burning garbage appears to be a simple answer to the garbage problem, but actually is not. The viewpoint states that burning waste maintains the public's wasteful attitude and pollutes the environment.

The meaning of *interred* can be determined by its use in context. What does *interred* mean?

The meaning of *perpetuates* can be determined by the context of the following few sentences. What does *perpetuates* mean?

"There is a war on—a war against waste," says Dr. Paul Connett, a chemistry professor at St. Lawrence University in Canton, New York. Dr. Connett believes that burning our garbage is *not* the way to win that war.

Burning garbage before dumping it in a landfill is a poor solution to the garbage problem. On the surface, it offers an easy, one-step way to get rid of the bulk of our garbage. All we need to do is take our trash to the shiny new waste incineration plant instead of to the dump. Machinery in the incineration plant puts the garbage into a furnace where forty-foot-high flames burn at two thousand degrees Fahrenheit. The high heat reduces the garbage to a pile of ashes, which can then be safely **interred** in a landfill. In this way, a great amount of trash becomes just a small amount of ash. Is this not a good way to make our landfills last longer?

If making landfills last longer were the only problem involved with managing our garbage, the answer to that question would be yes. But the burning of garbage is not as simple of a solution as it may seem. It is much more complicated.

First of all, accepting garbage burning as the solution to the waste problem **perpetuates** the attitude that we can unthinkingly use up our resources instead of wisely conserving them. This

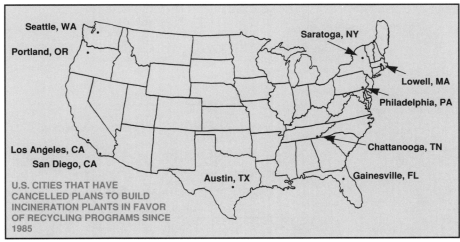

U.S. CITIES THAT HAVE CANCELLED PLANS TO BUILD INCINERATION PLANTS IN FAVOR OF RECYCLING PROGRAMS SINCE 1985

Source: *Environment* magazine

attitude holds that as long as we can find someplace to get rid of our garbage, we can keep living in the wasteful way we have always lived. But we cannot continue this attitude forever. Soon we will have cut down all our trees for making paper, and we will have taken out all the oil from the earth to make fuels and plastics. We must learn to create new life-styles that do not waste resources.

In addition to continuing a dangerous attitude about garbage, the waste-burning solution continues a dangerous practice as well—polluting the environment. Waste-burning plants produce toxic gases and ash. These by-products are either released into the atmosphere or buried in landfills where they seep into the water supply.

Finally, there are the invisible but deadly gases released from the smokestacks of the waste-burning plants. Judy Christup of Greenpeace, an international group of environmental activists, reports that an average waste-burning plant pours out 510 pounds of hydrocarbons, 5,000 pounds of lead, 361 pounds of cadmium, 20 pounds of mercury, and just over a half-pound of dioxin *every day*. Although the half-pound of dioxin is a small amount compared to the hundreds and even thousands of pounds of the other pollutants, it is the most poisonous of all.

There are many other reasons that building more waste-burning plants is the wrong answer to our garbage problem: the plants are expensive to build; they break down often; and they present a danger of explosions. They would reduce the amount of trash dumped into landfills, but such a reduction could be achieved by safer, more responsible methods. These include recycling and **minimizing** the amount of garbage we create in the first place. We must consider all the issues involved and not just take what seems to be the easy way out of our garbage problems.

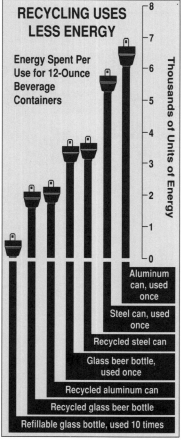

Source: Argonne National Laboratory

You learned the meaning of *minimize* in viewpoint 3. What does *minimizing* mean?

Do incinerators endanger the environment?

What dangers does a waste-burning plant pose to the environment, according to this viewpoint? Do you think such plants can be run safely? Why or why not?

minimize
residual
incinerated
generate
perpetuates
interred
stabilize

The words highlighted in viewpoints 3 and 4 are listed at the left. The short paragraphs below each are missing a word. Choose the word from the list that best completes each paragraph. You should be able to identify the appropriate word from its use in context.

1. The _____ ash left after burning garbage in waste-to-energy plants contains no more toxins than the garbage contained before it was burned.

2. The cost of dumping trash in landfills keeps rising. In order to _____ garbage disposal costs, other methods of trash disposal must be employed as well.

3. The volume of garbage is reduced by 90 percent after it has been _____ in a waste-burning plant.

4. People must _____ the amount of garbage they produce in the first place. This will help keep landfills from filling up so quickly.

5. Waste-to-energy plants can _____ electricity very cheaply without using up resources.

6. Although the ash from an incineration plant must still be _____ in a landfill, the amount of ash is far less than the original amount of garbage.

7. A wasteful attitude is the real cause of the garbage problem. This attitude _____ the problem. The problem will remain as long as the attitude is unchanged.

CHAPTER

PREFACE: Can Recycling Solve the Garbage Problem?

"Every day we share the earth and its resources with 250,000 more people than the day before," says Don Hinrichsen of the Natural Resources Defense Council in New York City. As the earth's population grows, food, water, land, and raw materials are needed to sustain it. Our planet has a limited supply of these natural resources. Conserving, not wasting, the earth's resources therefore becomes more important than ever before.

Most people realize that garbage contains large amounts of reusable materials. Many people argue that recycling discarded plastic, glass, paper, and metal conserves resources. They believe that recycling these materials would solve the garbage problem.

Other people argue that recycling alone cannot solve the garbage problem. They insist that incineration, landfills, and avoiding unnecessary waste must join recycling as workable weapons in the war on waste.

As you read, be alert to new words. Try to discover the meaning of the words from their context.

Editor's Note: The following viewpoint argues that recycling conserves natural resources and reduces garbage. It contends that recycling is the best solution for solving the garbage problem.

To solve the garbage problem, we must first recognize that garbage is just part of the larger problem of how to wisely manage our natural resources. The problem is not just on how to get rid of garbage, but how to get the most out of the limited resources we have, wasting as little as possible.

America's garbage grows daily while its natural resources **dwindle** daily. If we continue to use up our raw materials and bury what we have wasted, there soon will be only garbage left.

Each American discards 1,280 pounds of garbage every year, according to environmental researchers. This is an average arrived at by dividing the total amount of waste thrown away in the United States in a year by the number of people living here. David Morris of the Institute for Self-Reliance, an organization that favors self-supporting communities, notes that "a city the size of San Francisco (less than a million people) disposes of more aluminum than is produced by a small **bauxite** mine, more copper than a medium copper mine, and more paper than a good-sized timber stand." If all of this waste were recovered and reused, the bauxite and copper mines and timber forests would be conserved and landfills would last longer.

When we recycle, we save energy as well as materials. According to Cynthia Pollock-Shea of the Worldwatch Institute, an

The context is the clue to the meaning of *dwindle*. In the sentence, what is happening to the amounts of garbage is contrasted to what is happening to natural resources. From this context, then, what does *dwindle* mean?

What does the context tell you about *bauxite*. What is *bauxite*?

"Be fruitful and multiply and subdue the earth"

OKAY, NOW WHAT?

NOW TRY TO SITE A LANDFILL—

Toles. Copyright 1990 *The Buffalo News*. Reprinted with permission of Universal Press Syndicate. All rights reserved.

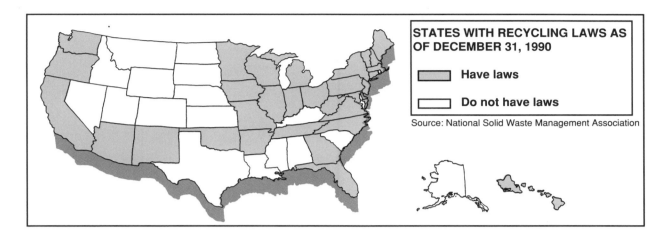

STATES WITH RECYCLING LAWS AS OF DECEMBER 31, 1990

Have laws

Do not have laws

Source: National Solid Waste Management Association

organization that studies environmental issues, making aluminum from recycled cans and other waste cuts energy use and air pollution by 95 percent. Pollock-Shea says that every aluminum soda pop can that is recycled saves the **equivalent** of 2 1/2 gallons of gasoline. So just recycling a six-pack of cola cans is like saving a tankful of gasoline for your car.

Likewise, says Pollock-Shea, recycling paper uses 75 percent less energy and 50 percent less water than making paper from wood pulp does. It also saves many trees. A paper mill that uses recycled paper can make new paper 50 to 80 percent more cheaply than a mill using wood pulp that has been newly cut down in the forest.

The Worldwatch Institute and other environmental groups believe that recycling is the best approach to solving America's garbage problem. In the words of Pollock-Shea, "Recycling offers communities everywhere the opportunity to trim their waste disposal needs, and thereby reduce disposal costs, while **simultaneously** combatting global environmental problems." So recycling solves two problems at the same time: how to deal with our garbage problem and how to protect and conserve our planet's natural resources.

Can you figure out the meaning of *equivalent* from its context? What does *equivalent* mean?

Simultaneously is defined within the context of this paragraph. What does *simultaneously* mean?

Does your family recycle?

What might prevent a family from recycling? Too much trouble? Lack of concern? If you and your family do not recycle, what would make you begin to recycle? Money? Concern for the environment? An easy way to do it? What do you think are good reasons for recycling?

Editor's Note: The following viewpoint argues that recycling cannot solve the garbage problem. Other methods also are needed to dispose of waste that cannot be recycled. The viewpoint states that a combination of methods for reducing garbage is best.

Myopic is defined in the next sentence. What does *myopic* mean?

You learned the word *incinerated* in viewpoint 3. What does *incinerator* mean?

Environmentally concerned people think that all we have to do is recycle all our waste and everything will be fine. They seem to believe that everything is recyclable—or should be—and that recycling alone will solve our garbage problems.

This is a **myopic** view of reality. Such nearsightedness prevents many people from seeing that there are really only four common materials that can be recycled: paper, cardboard, glass, and aluminum. Some plastic is being recycled also, but most types of plastic are not recyclable. What, then, do we do with all our other waste products?

Any realistic approach to dealing with our garbage—solid waste management, as it is called in the business—must consider a balanced program. Such a program uses recycling to recover usable material from discards, but it relies on other methods as well. These include resource recovery, source reduction, and landfills. Let us look at how these other methods work.

Resource recovery programs use waste-to-energy plants to recover energy from trash that would otherwise be buried in a landfill. Trash burned in the plants' **incinerators** creates heat. The heat is used to boil huge tanks of water to create steam. The steam can then be used to move the giant engines that produce electricity. When the city that produced the trash also uses the electricity from the waste-to-energy plant, the city has recovered a valuable resource. The city then does not have to buy as much electricity from a power company or burn as much coal to generate its own electricity. Thus it conserves natural resources as well.

SIBLING REVELRY   **Man Martin**

Sibling Revelry. Copyright 1990 Lew Little Ent. Reprinted with permission of Universal Press Syndicate. All rights reserved.

"Source reduction" means limiting the amount of garbage produced in the first place. The source of garbage is the many everyday products that we all use in our homes, schools, and workplaces. For example, we carry our groceries home in paper or plastic bags. Those bags usually become trash. They have done their job and we no longer need them, so we throw them away. We could (and should) recycle them. But if we had taken reusable cloth grocery bags to the supermarket and put our groceries in them, we would not have created any trash in the first place. We would have been using the source reduction method of helping to solve the garbage problem.

Finally, we will have to continue to use landfills to dispose of some of our garbage. For example, toxic or **hazardous** chemicals used in manufacturing cannot be burned or recycled. They must be carefully disposed of. Some people would say that we should not use such materials in the first place if they are that dangerous. But without such chemicals, many laborsaving, and even lifesaving, products may not be available for our use.

The Environmental Protection Agency (EPA) is the department of the federal government that enforces the laws made by Congress to protect the environment. It reports that only 11 percent of our waste is recycled. The EPA estimates that when cities begin operating official recycling programs, the percentage of waste recycled will be 25 percent. This still leaves 75 percent, or three-fourths, of all garbage to be disposed of by some other method.

William Ruckelshaus, a former head of the EPA, says, "It has been argued that we can recycle waste and reduce waste at the source to such an extent that our need for disposal **facilities** will disappear. But this is pie in the sky."

Recycling alone, or *any* one method alone for that matter, is not the answer to our garbage woes. Unless we use a combination of different methods to tackle our garbage problem, the problem will not be solved.

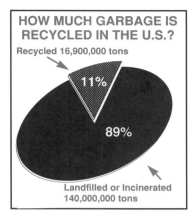

HOW MUCH GARBAGE IS RECYCLED IN THE U.S.?
Recycled 16,900,000 tons
11%
89%
Landfilled or Incinerated 140,000,000 tons

Source: Franklin Associates: 1986

What clues to the meaning of *hazardous* can you find in this paragraph? What does *hazardous* mean?

Can you determine the meaning of *facilities* from the context here? What does *facilities* mean?

Are many garbage-reduction methods needed?

Why does the author of this viewpoint believe that recycling alone cannot solve the garbage problem? The viewpoint mentions using cloth grocery bags as a way of reducing waste. What other reusable items could replace ones that are now thrown away?

Cartoonists express their opinions about current issues through pictures. The cartoonists often use words in their cartoons as well. Most of the words cartoonists use are easy to understand. Cartoonists want as many people as possible to enjoy their humor and to understand their cartoons. But sometimes cartoonists use words that are unfamiliar to the reader.

The cartoon below contains a few words that may be unfamiliar to you. These words are **decomposes**, **biodegradable**, and **self-righteousness**. Read the words in context, then try to determine their meanings. Next, check a dictionary to see if you have correctly understood the unfamiliar words. When you understand the meanings of the words, write a paragraph that tells in your own words what the cartoon means.

cathy®   **by Cathy Guisewite**

CHAPTER

PREFACE: Do Disposable Diapers Create a Garbage Problem?

To many people, disposable diapers are the symbol of what is wrong with America. They are wasteful, but people use them because they are convenient. Many environmentalists say that disposable diapers are the biggest cause of the garbage problem. Disposable diapers make up an unusually large portion of the garbage produced in America.

Many people, however, do not agree that disposable diapers are a real garbage problem. Using disposables does not endanger the environment any more than using cloth diapers, they say. Cloth diapers just present different, less obvious environmental problems.

Why does such a simple household item stir up such debate? The viewpoints in this chapter present arguments for and against the use of disposable diapers. As you read, try to determine the meaning of any new words you find by their context.

Disposable diapers create a garbage problem

Editor's Note: The following viewpoint argues that the huge number of disposable diapers thrown out each year has caused a garbage problem. It says that cloth diapers are a more environmentally responsible alternative.

Can you find the clues to the meaning of *comprised* in this paragraph? What does *comprised* mean?

From its context, what does *revolutionized* mean?

The disposable diaper appeared on the market in the late 1950s. By the 1970s disposables had cornered the diaper market. When Pampers® disposable diapers were first introduced in 1961, disposable diapers **comprised** less than 1 percent of all diapers sold in the United States. Today, disposable diapers are a $3.5 billion-a-year business making up nearly 85 percent of diaper sales. These convenient household items have saved families many hours of washing, drying, and folding baby diapers. In fact, disposable diapers have changed family life so much that the throwaway pads have been honored by the Smithsonian Institution in Washington, D.C., in an exhibit of inventions that have **revolutionized** our lives.

But can we afford the amount of garbage these diapers produce? We are a nation that is running out of landfill space in which to dump its garbage. Sixteen billion to 18 billion diapers are thrown away each year. That breaks down into 12,300 tons of diapers a day. And speaking of breaking down—disposable diapers do not. That is, the plastic-covered, chemically treated paper pads do not biodegrade in a landfill. Jeanne Wirka of the Environmental Action Foundation, an environmental research organization in Washington, D.C., notes, "The 18 billion disposable diapers Americans throw away each year . . . are choking up the nation's rapidly filling landfills."

Recently, diaper makers have marketed a biodegradable diaper.

Steve Artley: Reprinted with permission.

They want to make customers who are concerned about the environment to keep buying disposable diapers. But whether or not these new disposables actually do break down is a matter of debate. Colin Isaacs of the Pollution Probe Foundation, a Canadian environmental group, says that biodegradable diapers are just "the latest **gimmick**" by makers to calm the public's fears about a garbage crisis. Jeanne Wirka reports that there is "no evidence that biodegradable disposable diapers degrade any faster than [other] disposables."

The popularity of disposable diapers proves that Americans believe convenience is more important than ecology.

But environmentalists are trying to make us realize that such an attitude will hurt us in the long run. Disposables will cause a bigger problem in the future. And that future is **imminent**. The diapers take up much of the room in the landfills, and the landfills are filling up fast. Soon there will be nowhere to take the garbage, and we will be stuck with it.

Using things that can be reused again and again makes more sense than using something once and throwing it away. Environmentalists argue that using cloth diapers is safer—both for the environment and for a baby's well-being. Cloth diapers can be used again and again. They do not become garbage after a few hours' use like disposables do. Also, studies have shown that babies who wear cloth diapers get less diaper rash than babies who wear disposables.

Cloth diapers need to be cleaned of course, but parents can still save themselves the time needed to do this by sending the diapers out to a laundering service. Even when cleaned by a laundering service, cloth diapers are less expensive than disposables. Solid-waste expert Carl Lehrburger figures it this way: disposable diapers cost about twenty-two cents apiece; biodegradable ones can cost as much as thirty-nine cents each; while cloth ones that are cleaned by a laundering service cost about fifteen cents apiece. People who want an inexpensive, environmentally responsible, and convenient way to care for their babies should choose cloth diapers.

From the context, what is your understanding of the word *gimmick* as it is used here?

What are the clues to the meaning of *imminent*? What does *imminent* mean?

COSTS PER DIAPER BETWEEN CLOTH AND DISPOSABLES

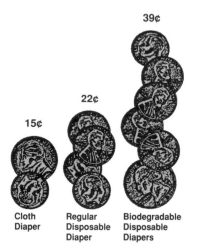

Cloth Diaper	Regular Disposable Diaper	Biodegradable Disposable Diapers
15¢	22¢	39¢

Source: National Association of Diaper Services

Are cloth diapers better than disposables?

Why are biodegradable disposable diapers no better for the environment than regular disposables, according to the viewpoint? What makes cloth diapers a better choice for babies and parents, in the author's view?

Editor's Note: Disposable diapers are not any more of a threat to the environment than cloth diapers are, argues this viewpoint. Disposables, it states, have been unfairly blamed for the garbage problem.

Most environmentalists insist that garbage is becoming a problem Americans are going to have to deal with soon. To focus the public's attention on the garbage problem, some environmentalists have focused their attack on, of all things, diapers.

Disposable diapers have become the villain in the story of our environment's destruction. Some environmentalists have blamed them for the current garbage problem. The environmentalists have made disposable diapers the symbol of an unthinking, wasteful America burying itself in its own trash.

Disposable diapers make up only 2 percent of the total amount of garbage in America. In comparison, yard waste—grass cuttings and raked leaves—**constitutes** 20 percent of the total waste volume. That is ten times as much waste as disposable diapers. Which is more necessary: caring for a lawn or caring for a baby?

Due to pressure by environmentalists, some people are going back to using cloth diapers. These people feel better about using a product that does not contribute to the environmental problem.

But these people are **deluded**. The belief that using cloth diapers saves the environment is false. According to *Newsweek* magazine's Robert Samuelson, if everyone switched to using cloth

A phrase that means the same thing as *constitutes* appears earlier in this paragraph. What does *constitutes* mean?

What are the clues to the meaning of *deluded*? What does *deluded* mean?

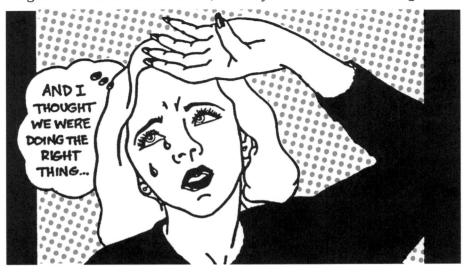

Anne Bullen for Environmental Action. Used with permission.

diapers, forty-three million diapers per day would have to be washed and dried. They would have to be washed in hot water and dried in hot-air dryers. That means using fuel—gas or electricity—to heat the air and water and run the machines. In order to make using cloth diapers as convenient as using disposables, most people would hire a diaper service to launder the diapers. This means even more fuel used and more air pollution because these services use delivery trucks to pick up and return diapers.

So, we see that changing from disposable diapers to cloth ones does not save the environment. It just changes the way the environment is damaged. Some environmentalists admit this. For example, Allen Hershkowitz of the Natural Resources Defense Council, a major environmental group, says: "We simply can't say that disposables are terrible and reusable diapers are great for the environment. . . . Whatever the choice, there are environmental costs."

Making disposable diapers the bad guys in the garbage crisis does not help solve the problem. It **hinders** the search for real solutions. The problem cannot be solved by blaming one item and banning its use. We simply have to choose how we want to handle the garbage we do create, and then follow through with our decision.

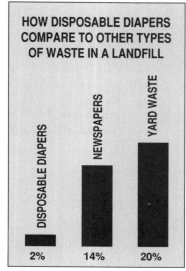

HOW DISPOSABLE DIAPERS COMPARE TO OTHER TYPES OF WASTE IN A LANDFILL

DISPOSABLE DIAPERS 2%   NEWSPAPERS 14%   YARD WASTE 20%

Source: *Newsweek* & *Garbage*

How does the context help you determine the meaning of *hinders* here? What does *hinders* mean?

Do cloth diapers endanger the environment?

How does using cloth diapers affect the environment, according to the viewpoint? After reading viewpoints 7 and 8, which type of diaper would you choose for your child? Why?

Recognizing and Defining Cognates

A cognate is a word that comes from a similar word. The cognate is usually a different part of speech than the word it is taken from. For example, the word *conserve* is a verb, an action word. It means "to avoid wasteful use" of something. To conserve water, for example, is to not waste it, but to use it only as needed. The noun form of *conserve* is the cognate *conservation*. It means the act or idea of conserving something. To continue the above example, when we do not waste water, we are practicing water *conservation*.

Recognizing cognates enables a reader to determine the meanings of many unfamiliar words. For example, a reader may know what *conserve* means, but may not have ever seen the word *conservation*. When the reader sees the word *conservation* for the first time, he or she can figure out the meaning of *conservation* if he or she recognizes it as a cognate of *conserve*. Being able to recognize cognates increases a reader's skill in understanding new words.

The following sentences use cognates of the new words that were highlighted in the viewpoints of this chapter. In the blank space before each sentence write the highlighted word from which the cognate is taken. Then determine the meaning of the cognate.

Highlighted words from this chapter are:

comprised   revolutionized
gimmick   constitutes
deluded   hinders

_____ 1. Disposable diapers have had a **revolutionary** effect on the role of women in America.

      Revolutionary means:

_____ 2. The **constitution** of a landfill's contents is 90 percent paper.

      Constitution means:

_____ 3. The belief that using cloth diapers is better for the environment is a **delusion**.

      Delusion means:

_____ 4. Blaming diapers for the garbage problem is a **hindrance** to finding a solution to the problem.

      Hindrance means: